PIANO FOR ADULTS

LEVEL THREE

by WESLEY SCHAUM

Teacher Consultants: Alfred Cahn, Joan Cupp, Sue Pennington

INDEX

SCHAUM PUBLICATIONS, INC.

10235 N. Port Washington Rd.   Mequon, WI 53092
© Copyright 1993 by Schaum Publications, Inc., Mequon, Wisconsin
International Copyright Secured   All Rights Reserved
Printed in U.S.A.

01-53
HE-2

FOREWORD

This method is tailored for an older individual — adult or teen-ager. It may also be used for mature students of a younger age.

The progress here is much more gradual than other adult methods. This allows the student to be entirely comfortable with the learning steps. The rate of progress is flexible; work in this book can be leisurely or fast paced, depending upon the individual pupil and preference of the teacher.

The musical excerpts are themes from symphonies, operas, ballets, concertos, oratorios, chamber music, vocal and choral literature. Also included are folk songs from many ethnic groups. No simplified *piano* music is used. Music appreciation stories of the musical and biographical information and portraits of the composers are provided.

Systematic review of the various learning elements is provided by a planned variety of key signatures, time signatures, tempos and musical styles. This enhances the educational appeal and provides a series of modest challenges to the student.

A minimum of finger numbers are used. Various changed and extended hand positions are used to avoid becoming locked into a rigid five-finger position.

A reference page, correlating notes and keyboard position along with basic musical symbols, is found on the front inside cover and continued on the back inside cover. A music dictionary, appropriate for level three, is provided on pages 46-47. The index on page 48 helps to locate explanations contained within the method.

MUSICIANSHIP CURRICULUM

Sound musicianship is attained by thorough musical study, and staying on each level until it is mastered. It is intended that this method book be part of a systematic approach to learning to play the piano. This is done by working in four books at the same level before moving up to the next level.

1. Method 2. Theory 3. Technic 4. Repertoire

This 4-book curriculum may be tailored to each individual student, depending on age, ability and interests. Here are the Schaum supplements available at this level. At least one book should be assigned in each category, with preference to the first title in each group:

THEORY Books:	THEORY WORKBOOK, Level 3 (see back inside cover) RHYTHM WORKBOOK, Level 3 ARPEGGIO SPELLER
TECHNIC Books:	FINGERPOWER, Level 3 AROUND THE WORLD IN ALL KEYS (scales cadences & pieces) CZERNY IN ALL KEYS, Book 2
REPERTOIRE Books:	CLASSIC THEMES, Book 2 CHRISTMAS SOLOS, Level 3 EASY BOOGIE, Book 2 HANSEL and GRETEL PETER and the WOLF RHYTHM and BLUES, Book 2

SHEET MUSIC May Also Be Used For REPERTOIRE - see page 47.
Optional Book Featuring CHORD SYMBOLS and IMPROVISING:
EASY KEYBOARD HARMONY, Book 2

(All Books are Published by Schaum Publications, Inc.)
For additional suggestions of supplementary books and sheet music solos, ask for a free copy of the "Schaum Teachers Guide."

CONTENTS

"Correcting" Wrong Notes

When learning and practicing a new piece, a common reaction is to "correct" any wrong notes by immediately stopping and playing the proper note. While this trains the ear to listen for the correct sound, unfortunately it interrupts the rhythm. The first several times you practice a piece you will probably need to make some "corrections." Therefore, it is best to practice extremely slowly, so the correct notes can be played *while maintaining a steady beat.* If you hear a note that sounds wrong, first look at the music to be sure you have the correct note by checking the key signature and prior accidentals. (Sometimes it may *sound* wrong but may be an intentional dissonance.) When you have played a wrong note, it is best to go back to the beginning of a phrase and play it again, this time with the correct note. If necessary, repeat the *entire phrase* several times very slowly to reinforce in your mind the correct notes with the correct rhythm.

Immediately stopping to "correct" wrong notes is a BAD HABIT during practice, which easily becomes a BAD HABIT in playing. Most listeners, even non-musicians, can detect an *interruption* in the flow of the music. An occasional wrong note may often go unnoticed unless you stop to "correct" it. Stopping to re-strike the correct note disrupts the rhythm and calls undue attention to the wrong note.

Your Repertoire

Repertoire (reh-per-TWAR) is defined as musical compositions previously studied, mastered, and currently maintained by a musician or musical group, so that performance can be given with a minimum of preparation. Professional musicians, ranging from a church organist to a supper club pianist, have several hundred pieces in their repertoire. Likewise, symphony orchestras, ballet companies and even rock groups have a substantial repertoire.

Part of the pleasure of piano study is sharing with others the music you have learned. Try to develop a small repertoire so that you have several pieces prepared when your friends ask to hear you play. A repertoire should represent your current best efforts. Select pieces which you really enjoy playing and which feel very comfortable to you. Although it is preferable to have the pieces memorized, if you don't feel confident, it is better to use your music.

A repertoire of two or three short pieces is probably sufficient, unless you like to do a lot of performing. The selections can change if you tire of them or find something you like better. It's a good idea to play all of your repertoire pieces several times each week as part of your daily review.

Value of Review

The first phase of learning a piece of music deals with the basics of correct notes, rhythm, fingering, dynamics, pedal, etc. At this level it usually takes from one to four weeks, depending upon the amount and effectiveness of your practice time. It is normal for some pieces to be learned quickly while others take more time. Obviously, as the music becomes more difficult, the preparation time gets longer. You may often reach a plateau where the piece can be played all right, yet there may be areas that are a little weak or cannot be done with consistent accuracy. At this point your performance may be rated as *satisfactory* or *good* but not *very good* or *excellent.* Your teacher will determine when the first phase is finished and may recommend that practice be discontinued temporarily.

Review Phase. After several weeks, your teacher may ask you to review a piece which has already gone through the first phase. The time spent for this review usually has a specific purpose. For example, if there were parts containing wrong notes, some hesitations, or a few measures where the tempo slows down, these should be improved and refined during the review phase. Memorization can be accomplished during review. Review time is also an opportunity to gain confidence in your playing and to add a piece to your repertoire.

Use of a Cassette Recorder

Occasional use of a cassette recorder can be very helpful. Your own playing sounds quite different from the perspective of a recording. You may hear and identify things that you overlooked as you were playing. This is an excellent way to improve your critical listening skills. It is good to make and listen to a recording of your own playing once or twice a month, or more often if recommended by your teacher.

A cassette recorder can also be used for duet practice. You or your teacher can record one of the duet parts, then play the other part along with the recording to hear the complete duet.

Most "boom-box" style cassette players have one or two built-in microphones for recording. These recorders include an electronic circuit used as an automatic volume control. It increases the volume of low level sounds and reduces the volume of loud sounds. Unfortunately, this is not good for recording music because it narrows the range of loudness. Instead of a normal dynamic range of **pp** to **ff**, it will sound more like **p** to **f**. Be aware of this when listening to recordings made on this type of machine.

If your cassette player is a component of a home stereo system you probably will have to purchase a separate microphone. First, check the cassette instruction booklet to be sure it can accommodate a microphone. If so, you will need to know the type of microphone, type of plug needed (at the end of the microphone wire) and where to insert the plug. Inexpensive microphones are available at electronic supply stores like Radio Shack and at many music stores and record stores.

The microphone may be placed on top of the piano, in the center, using a folded towel to avoid vibration. If the wire is not long enough, the microphone should be placed as close to the piano as possible. You don't need a stand for the microphone; place it on a TV tray or card table using a folded towel as a cushion. The top of the microphone should be facing the piano and positioned so it is about equally distant from the ends of the keyboard, otherwise the balance between bass and treble will be affected. If you do not have a cassette machine at home, you may be able to borrow one. Your teacher may also make an occasional recording during your lesson.

Recording With A Digital Piano

Many digital pianos and some electronic keyboards have a built-in recorder called a sequencer. This makes a digital recording of your playing. Unless your instrument has a special diskette drive for saving such recordings, the recording will be preserved only as long as the instrument is plugged in, although the power switch can be off. The duration of the digital recording is limited by the amount of electronic "memory" built into the instrument. Some instruments have two recording channels which enable you to "layer" one recording on top of another. Refer to the instructions that accompanied your instrument.

Stars and Stripes Forever (Sousa)

DIRECTIONS: There are several changes of hand position in this piece. Be sure to follow the fingering carefully.
Learn to play the notes with correct rhythm first, then, practice the left hand alone with pedal, before playing this piece as written.

JOHN PHILIP SOUSA (SOO-zah) 1854-1932 — United States

On Christmas Eve of 1896, on board a ship returning from a vacation in Italy, Sousa composed the "Stars and Stripes Forever." It was first performed two days later. It has become famous all over the world, is one of the most popular marches ever written and was one of Sousa's personal favorites.

Slurs and Phrase Marks

A **slur** is a curved line placed over or under groups of notes to be played legato. Slurs are found more frequently in the accompaniment, and often indicate notes forming broken chords and other accompaniment patterns. Various slurred groups are found in the bass clef of this piece.

The same curved line may also be a **phrase mark**. A phrase mark is usually longer than a slur and may extend two or more measures. Phrase marks are found more commonly in the melody and are used in the treble clef of this piece. Notes within the phrase are to be played legato. In more advanced music it is difficult and sometimes impossible to distinguish between a slur and a phrase mark.

Slurs and phrase marks make it easier to recognize patterns and note groups. It is important that you *train your eye to pick out note groups which are the same or similar.* Melodic segments which recur give a clue to the form of a piece. Accompaniment patterns are often repeated. All of this is very helpful in learning and memorizing a piece of music.

Theme from 4th Symphony (Mendelssohn, Op. 90, 1st Movement)

DIRECTIONS: If necessary, practice hands separately first. Start with a slower metronome speed, around 60, and gradually increase over a period of at least one week, until the performance speed is reached. The pedal should be added only after both hands can be played together with ease.

Broken chords, indicated with slurs, are printed in red. These same chords are used many times.

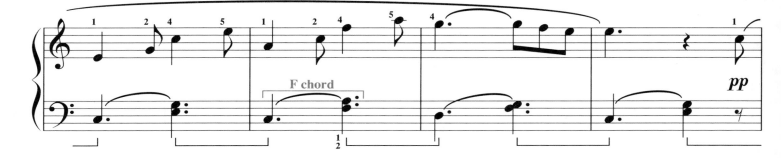

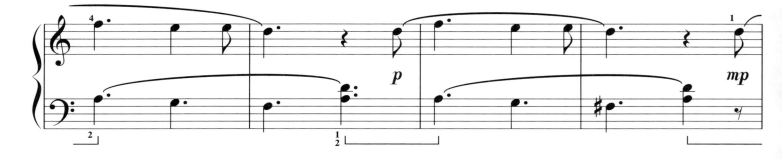

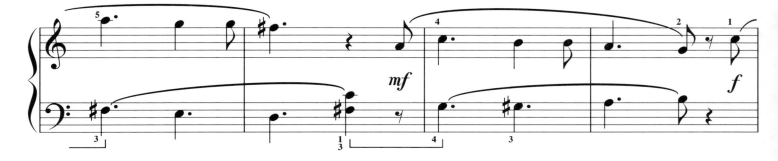

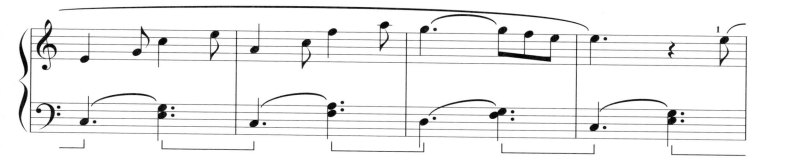

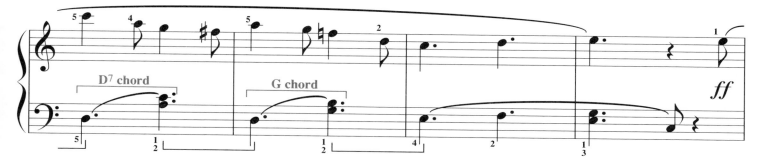

FELIX MENDELSSOHN (MEN-dell-sohn) 1809-1847 — Germany

Mendelssohn grew up in a wealthy household where music and the arts were promoted. His family home had a room large enough to seat 100 people, where many private recitals and plays were performed. He was a child prodigy, and wrote several string symphonies by age 12. At age 17, he wrote incidental music to the Shakespeare play "A Midsummer Night's Dream." The wedding march from this music, commonly used as a recessional, is probably his most famous composition. His violin concerto, opus 64, continues to be among the most popular in the repertoire. He also wrote chamber music, choral music, numerous piano solos titled "Songs Without Words," and five symphonies for full orchestra.

The 4th Symphony, known as the "Italian Symphony," was composed after Mendelssohn spent nine months in various cities in Italy. It was first performed in London in 1833.

Schaum's **Theory Workbook, Level 3** provides written work coordinated with this book to reinforce the learning elements.

Leger Line Notes
This piece has many notes written on leger lines. Refer to the front inside cover to identify any notes you do not know.

La Cucaracha * (Mexican Folk Song)

DIRECTIONS: At the beginning, the notes for the left hand are written in treble clef. Watch for the change of clef eight measures before the end. The left hand notes in the final eight measures are the same as in the first eight measures, except that they are written in the bass clef. The entire accompaniment consists of three different chord patterns; can you find them?

* La Cucaracha means "cockroach" in Spanish.

The Trout ("Die Forelle") (Schubert, D-550*)

DIRECTIONS: This piece uses several groups of 16th notes. The counting numbers have been printed in RED. Watch particularly for the 16th note rhythm in the last line of music.

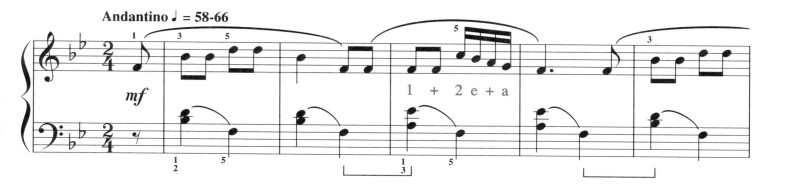

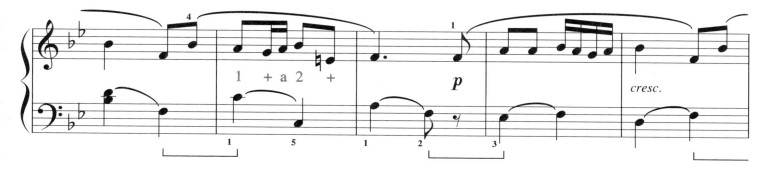

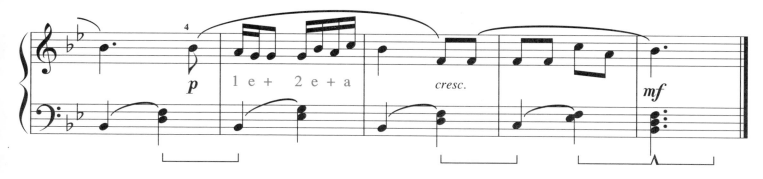

FRANZ SCHUBERT (SHOO-burt) 1797-1828 — Austria

Schubert wrote hundreds of songs using poems by friends and by outstanding poets of his day, such as Goethe and Schiller. Schubert's expertise was making the musical mood and style of the accompaniment fit the poetry. His songs are called art songs (lieder, in German) because of the quality of the music.

Schubert's best-known song probably is "Ave Maria," used in the classic Walt Disney film, "Fantasia," available on videotape. He is also famous for his 8th symphony, known as the "Unfinished," which many consider to be his finest work.

*Because most of Schubert's music remained unpublished for many years after his death, the few opus numbers used at that time were not adequate. D-550 (see title, at top of page) is a number assigned to this music by Otto Erich Deutsch, who cataloged all of Schubert's compositions. "The Trout," although written in 1817, was not published until 1895.

8th Note Triplets

A triplet is a group of three notes of equal value. The three notes of a triplet fit into the same time-span as two notes of the same value. In this piece, the three notes of an 8th note triplet fit into <u>one beat</u>.

Triplets are usually indicated by a slur and an italic number 3. However, in a piece with many triplets, the slur and italic 3 are often indicated only with the first few note groups, as is done in this piece. Thereafter, three 8th notes beamed together indicate a triplet. In some music, the slur and 3 are not used even at the beginning. In time signatures where the quarter note gets one count, it is then assumed that three 8th notes beamed together are a triplet.

A variation of the triplet occurs on the 3rd count in measure 11; the *first two notes of the triplet are tied*.

Beautiful Dreamer (Foster)

DIRECTIONS: Before playing the notes, count and tap the rhythm for the first line of music. <u>This should be done with the supervision of your teacher.</u> (See the teachers note below, for suggestions.) It is very important that the triplet notes be played with the correct rhythm before starting to practice. Using a metronome may be helpful. You may want to practice the right hand alone at first. Add the pedal after you have learned to play hands together.

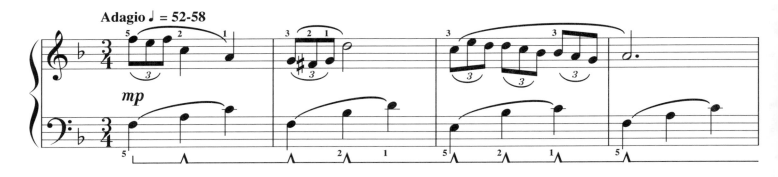

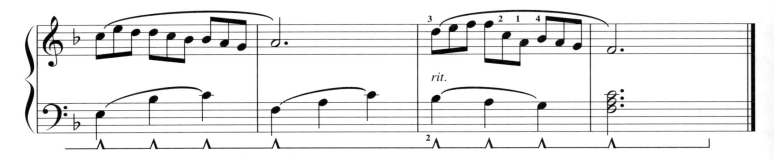

Teacher's Note: Because of different ways of teaching, the counting of triplet groups has purposely been left to the preference of the teacher. As a suggestion, you could use: "one-trip-let," "two-trip-let," etc. (the spoken number, of course, would depend upon the number of the beat). Saying a three syllable word such as "trip-oh-let," "beau-ti-ful," or "choc-o-late" often helps the student to feel the triplet rhythm. Setting a metronome to click each note of a triplet may also be helpful.

Valse Lente from "Coppelia" (Delibes)

DIRECTIONS: As a preparatory, count and tap the treble clef in the first line of music. Be careful to differentiate between the two 8th notes on the 3rd beat of measure 2 and the triplet which follows. The same rhythm occurs in the second line of music. Notice that some of the broken chords in the accompaniment are used more than once.

Watch for two wide intervals (octave and 7th) in the melody, from the last note of the second line through the 3rd measure of the third line. The damper pedal helps to achieve a legato phrase where these wide intervals occur.

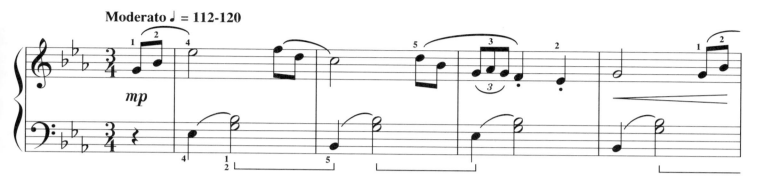

LEO DELIBES (dah-LEEB) 1836-1891 — France

Delibes is known primarily for two ballets, "Coppelia" and "Sylvia." "Coppelia," written in 1870, is one of the best-loved in the entire ballet repertory and is frequently performed by American ballet companies. It tells the story of Franz, a young man who falls in love with the beautiful Coppelia, whom he has seen only from below her balcony. His fiance, Swanilda, is jealous and sneaks into Coppelia's house to find out more about her. Swanilda and her friends discover that Coppelia is a life-sized mechanical doll! After an adventurous escape from the house, Swanilda and Franz are reconciled and the ballet ends in a wedding festival.

Schaum's **Fingerpower, Level 3** provides basic technic exercises to strengthen fingers and develop dexterity.

Key Signature: A Major

The three sharps used in this key signature mean that all F's, C's and G's are sharp. The key signature eliminates the need to write a sharp sign for every F, C and G.

Foggy, Foggy Dew (American Folk Ballad)

DIRECTIONS: As a preparatory, play the A major scale on page 25. The chord patterns, A, D6 and E7, which are used in the first three measures, are repeated in various combinations to form the entire accompaniment. Be sure to remember the three sharps in the key signature.

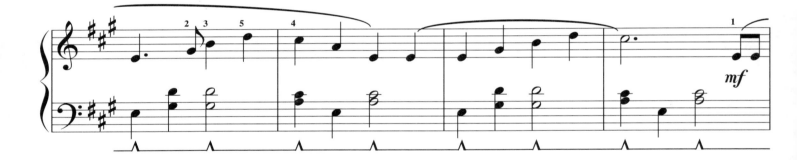

Each line of lyrics corresponds to a phrase in the melody.

When I was a bach'lor I lived all alone,
I worked at the weaver's trade.
But one fine day in May I met a sweet girl,
And I wooed that fair young maid.

And I wooed her in the summer time,
and in the winter too,
There were very many times that I held her in my arms
Just to keep her from the foggy foggy dew.

Key Signature: E Major

The *first three sharps* of this key signature, F, C and G, are the same as for the key of A Major (see page 12). The *fourth sharp* is D. In the Key of E Major, all F's, C's, G's and D's are sharp.

Parallel Motion

When the right hand and left hand move together in the same direction with the same intervals, up or down, it is called *parallel motion*. This piece has several measures, marked with red, where both hands play the same notes one or two octaves apart in parallel motion.

The Heavens Are Telling (Beethoven, Op. 48, No. 4)

DIRECTIONS: As a preparatory, play the E Major scale on page 25. Be sure to play all F's, C's, G's and D's sharp, as indicated by the key signature.

D.C. al fine, in the last measure, means to go back to the beginning and repeat, ending in the measure with the word *fine*. D.C. al fine will be found in the dictionary on page 46.

LUDWIG VAN BEETHOVEN (BAY-toe-ven) 1770-1827—Germany
Although most famous for his nine symphonies, Beethoven also wrote many pieces of piano, choral, and vocal music. "Die Ehre Gottes aus der Natur," the original German title, is part of a set of six songs written around 1802 in Vienna. Although translated here as "The Heavens Are Telling," it is also sometimes called "The Heavens Declare His Glory." This song was dedicated to a nobleman, Count von Browne, who may have commissioned the music.

Changing Fingers On The Same Note

In measures 7 and 15 you will find double finger numbers 3-5, above the treble staff. This means to play the note at first with the 3rd finger, then while holding the key down, change to the 5th finger. There is to be no interruption of the rhythm while making this finger change.

Theme from Overture to "The Marriage of Figaro" (Mozart)

DIRECTIONS: The notes in the last 8 measures are the same as the first 8 measures, except they are played one octave higher and the left hand is written in treble clef. Only the final three notes of the accompaniment are different.

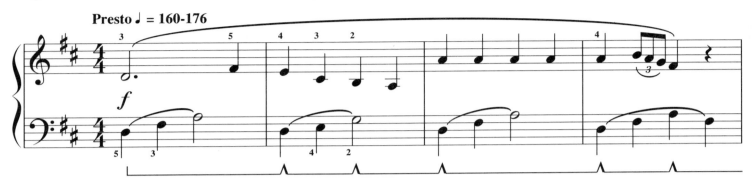

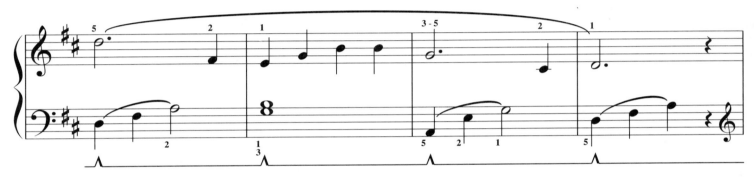

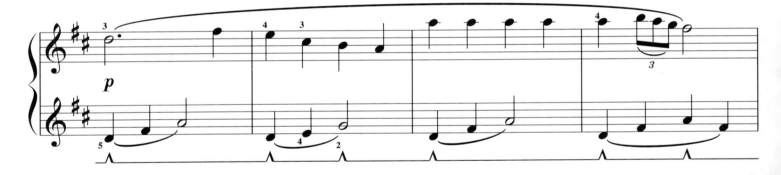

WOLFGANG AMADEUS MOZART (MOE-tsart) 1756-1791 — Austria

Mozart is one of the world's most famous and beloved composers. "Amadeus," the popular academy-award-winning movie about his life, available on video tape, greatly expanded the public appreciation of Mozart's music and his genius. Excerpts from "The Marriage of Figaro" appeared in the movie.

An **overture** (OH-ver-tshoor) is a musical introduction to a larger work such as an opera, operetta, musical play, oratorio or drama. It usually establishes the mood for the opening scene. An overture is often performed as a separate unit on a concert program. The overture to "The Marriage of Figaro" is unusual in that it does *not* use any themes which appear in the opera itself.

"The Marriage of Figaro" is a comedy involving the secret romances of several couples of different social classes. Jealousy spawns a plot involving disguises and trickery. All couples are happily reconciled at the end. It was first performed in 1786.

Review: Sharp Key Signatures

The sequence of sharps in any key signature is always the same. Sharps are named from left to right: F# — C# — G# — D#.
The first sharp (farthest to the left) is always F#. The second sharp is always C#. The third sharp is always G#, etc.

The two sharps (F# and C#) used in the key signature for D major on page 14 are the *same as the first two sharps* used in the key signature for E major on this page.

Cielito Lindo (Beautiful Heaven) (Fernandez)

DIRECTIONS: The slurs in the bass clef indicate broken chord patterns for the accompaniment. In the first 7 measures, the same broken chord is played twice in each measure. The last 8 measures have a variation of the same accompaniment. As shown by the slurs, each measure uses the *same three notes* in two different broken chord patterns.

Measures 4, 6, and 7 have a tie beneath the phrase mark. These ties create a syncopation and are indicated with red. Similar ties occur in the last two lines of music.

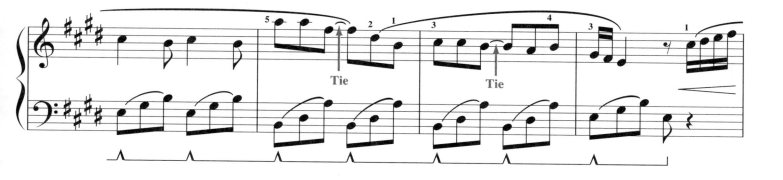

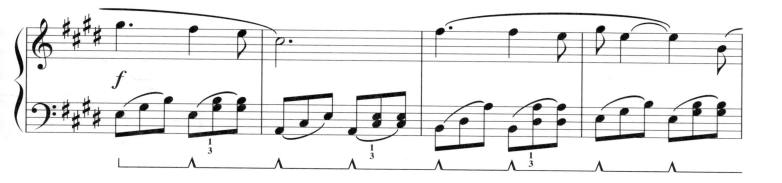

Review of Transposing

To transpose means to play in a different key. The theme in the key of F major used in the first 8 measures, is transposed to the key of A major and repeated in the second 8 measures. The counting, intervals, fingering and pedal patterns remain the same; only the notes change.

Theme from String Quartet No. 2, (2nd Movement) (Borodin)

DIRECTIONS: A double bar in the middle of a piece is a warning to alert you of a change, either of key signature or of time signature. Watch for double bars at the end of measures 8 and 16.

The slurs in the left hand indicate various broken chord patterns, many of which are repeated.

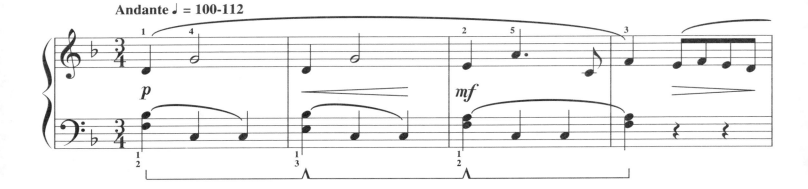

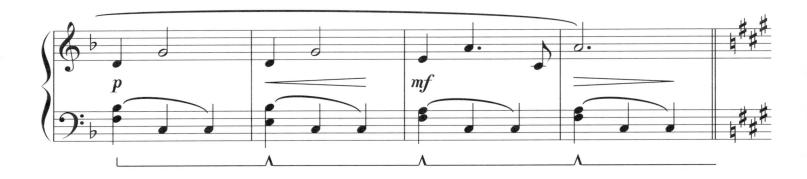

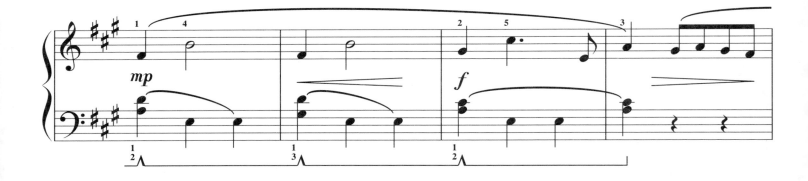

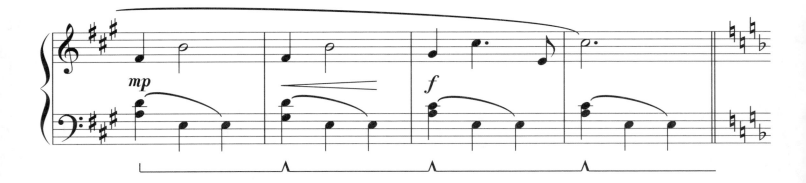

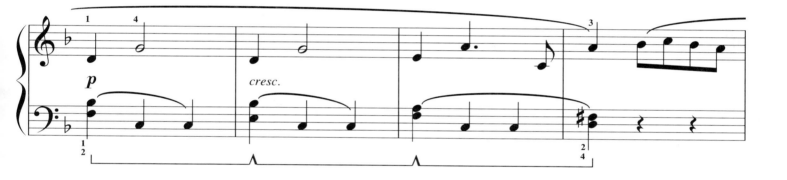

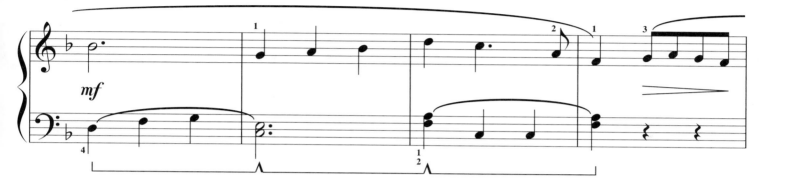

ALEXANDER BORODIN (BOH-roe-deen) 1833-1887 — Russia

Borodin received extensive training in music as a boy ,and wrote his first composition at age 14. Although his profession was that of a chemist and scientist, he was an accomplished performer on several instruments. Since he devoted only spare time to music, he composed quite slowly and his output was small.

Borodin's most ambitious work is the opera "Prince Igor," started 18 years before he died, and completed by two musical colleagues after his death. He also wrote three symphonies and a small amount of piano, vocal and chamber music.

Borodin is best known to American audiences for the music used in the Broadway show and movie "Kismet." This show incorporates Borodin's themes from various works, including "Prince Igor" and the 2nd String Quartet. In "Kismet," the theme used on this page is titled "Baubles, Bangles and Beads." The 2nd String Quartet, from which it came, was written in 1881 and was dedicated to his wife.

Minor Key

This piece is in the key of D minor. D minor is *related* to F major because they *both have the same key signature* (one flat). The related key, F major, is used on page 17.

Syncopation

Syncopation is a style of rhythm where the accent is between the normal beats. The note group, 8th-quarter-8th, is a common syncopation. It is used in measure 2 and in many other measures that follow.

Joshua Fit the Battle of Jericho (African-American Spiritual)

DIRECTIONS: As a preparatory, count and tap the treble clef rhythm with right hand, using a slow metronome speed (around 80). Counting numbers are printed in red. For extra practice, add the bass clef rhythm, tapped with left hand. If helpful, use pencil to write additional counting numbers.

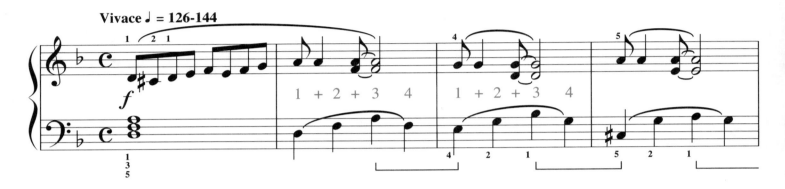

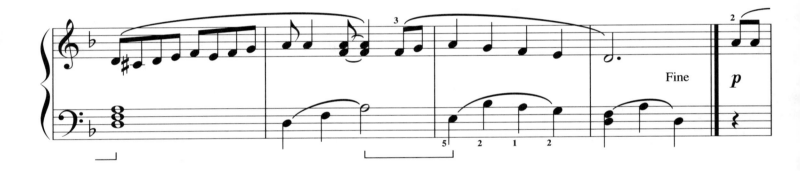

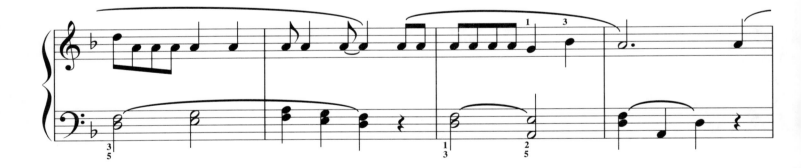

Review of Repeat With 1st and 2nd Endings

The 1st ending begins in measure 9 and continues up to the repeat sign at the end of measure 16. After playing measure 16, go back to the beginning and play again through measure 8, then skip to the 2nd ending (measure 17) and continue playing to the end.

The Lark (Glinka)

DIRECTIONS: This piece is in the key of B minor. It is related to the key of D major because both have the same key signature. The bass clef slurs indicate broken chord accompaniment patterns, many of which are used several times.

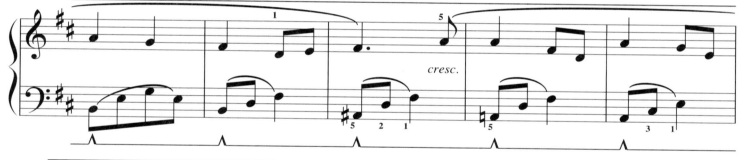

MIKHAIL GLINKA (GLIN-kah) 1804-1857 — Russia

Glinka is not well-known outside of his native country. However, his two operas established a unique Russian style which greatly influenced other Russian composers, especially Tchaikowsky and Mussorgsky.

Glinka also composed a small amount of chamber music and over 80 songs. "The Lark" is one in a set of 12 songs collectively titled "A Farewell to St. Petersburg," written in 1840.

20

Cut Time (2/2)
"Cut Time" is a common name given to the 2/2 time signature. There are two counts per measure. A *half note* gets one count. The symbol for cut time is (𝄵). It is also sometimes called *alla breve* (ah-lah-BREV). Note values are as follows:

♩ = 1 Count   ♪ ♪ = 1 Count   ♫♫ = 1 Count   𝅝 = 2 Counts

Erie Canal (American Folk Song)

DIRECTIONS: The metronome numbers are for half notes because the half note gets one count in this piece. Counting numbers are printed in red for the first line of music. Notice especially the counting used for 8th notes.

The slurs in the bass clef indicate accompaniment patterns, many of which are used several times. This piece is in the key of G minor. It is related to B-flat major because both have the same key signature. This piece purposely uses no pedal.

The musical form is A-A¹-B-A². The treble clef phrases determine the form. The first two phrases are the A section. The next two phrases are the A¹ section. The last two phrases are the A² section. There are slight variations in the melody of each A section. The accompaniment for all three A sections is the same.

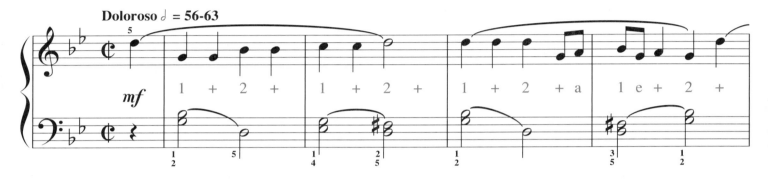

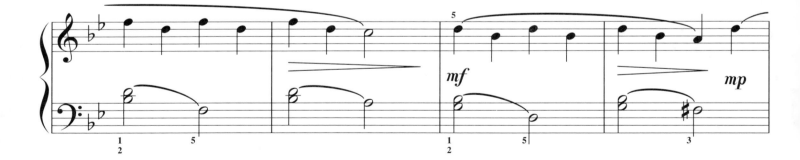

White Key Sharp

A sharp means to go one key to the right. In most cases this is to be a black key. However, E sharp is a white key because there is no black key immediately to the right of E. E sharp is played the same as F.

Divided Measure at the Change of Key

This piece changes key after the 3rd count of measure 8. To make the change of key more clear, and to coincide with the key change at end of the piece, only the first 3 counts of measure 8 appear on the second line. The 4th count of measure 8 is on the third line. The counting for this measure is printed in red. There should be no delay or interruption between the 3rd and 4th counts.

Sans Souci Polka (Strauss, Op. 178)

DIRECTIONS: This piece is in cut time. See page 20 for an explanation of the counting.

There are two changes of key, one at the end of the second line, and another at the end of the fourth line.

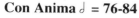

JOHANN STRAUSS, JR. (STROWS) 1825 - 1899 — Austria

Strauss was a popular dance orchestra leader in Vienna. He and his musicians were in constant demand at large dance halls, and for special social occasions. He toured Europe and Russia with his orchestra, and became known as the "Waltz King" because of the large number of waltzes which he wrote. His father and two brothers were also dance orchestra leaders and composers.

Often forgotten is that Strauss also wrote over 100 polkas which were frequently played by his orchestra. The polka "Sans Souci" (san SOO-see), meaning "carefree," was written in 1856.

Strauss visited the United States in 1872, as guest conductor of an enormous International Peace Jubilee in Boston, where 20,000 singers and 10,000 musicians were combined. 100 assistant-conductors were needed to coordinate the massive group.

Hold (Fermata) 🎵

This symbol, when placed above any note, interval or chord, means to hold a little longer than the normal time value, at the discretion of the performer . It makes a temporary pause in the normal flow of rhythm.

Change of Time Signature

This piece has a change of time signature along with a new tempo mark and metronome speed in measure 9.

Themes from Romanian Rhapsody No. 1 (Enesco, Op. 11)

DIRECTIONS: Watch for the hold in measure 8. Extend the sound briefly before going on to the next measure.
   Be sure to observe the new time signature and tempo in measure 9.

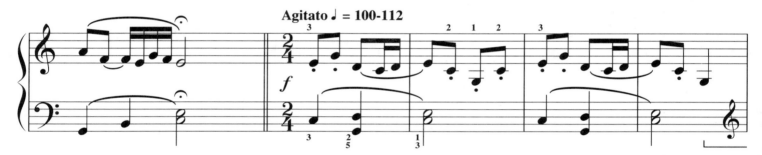

GEORGE ENESCO (en-ESS-koh) 1881-1955 — Romania

Enesco was a talented composer, conductor, teacher and virtuoso violin soloist, who pioneered the development of a national style of music in Romania. He promoted operas, concerts and recitals. He encouraged young composers by establishing the Enesco Prize and the Romanian Composers Society. Enesco visited the United States several times, appearing as guest conductor and soloist with the Philadelphia Orchestra and the New York Philharmonic Orchestra.

   The "Romanian Rhapsody No. 1," written when he was 20 years old, is probably his best known work. He also wrote an opera, three symphonies, three orchestral suites and three violin sonatas.

Key Signature: A-flat Major

The *first three flats* of this key signature, B, E and A, are the <u>same as for the key of E-flat major</u> (see page 11). The *fourth flat* is D. In the key of A-flat major, all B's, E's, A's and D's are flat. These four flats spell the word B-E-A-D.

Lullaby ("Wiegenlied") (Brahms, Op. 49, No. 4)

DIRECTIONS: As a preparatory, play the scale of A-flat major (see page 24).
Be sure to play all B's, E's, A's and D's flat, as indicated by the key signature. Watch for the 16th notes near the end.

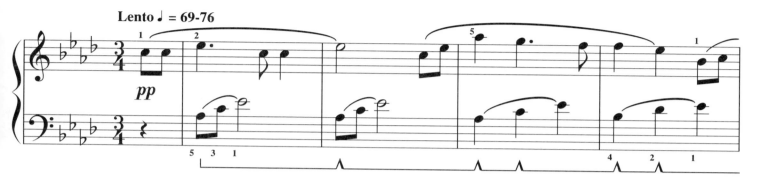

JOHANNES BRAHMS (BRAHMS) 1833-1897 — Germany
Brahms is one of the famous "Three B's" of music: Bach, Beethoven and Brahms. All were German composers who lived at different times, Bach was born in 1685 and Beethoven in 1770. All wrote music of very high quality.

Brahms' substantial reputation is based on his orchestral music (4 symphonies, 2 piano concertos and a violin concerto) along with numerous chamber music and solo piano compositions. He also wrote a large quantity of vocal and choral music.

The Lullaby ("Wiegenlied" in German) is one of a set of five songs for voice and piano, written in 1868. This simple melody, known to millions, is one of his best known themes.

Key Signatures With Flats

Flats in a key signature are numbered from *left to right*. The flats are always in the *same order*.

1 Flat =
Key of F Major

2 Flats =
Key of B-flat Major

3 Flats =
Key of E-flat Major

4 Flats =
Key of A-flat Major

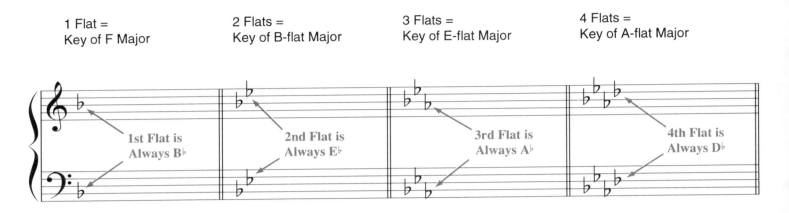

1st Flat is
Always B♭

2nd Flat is
Always E♭

3rd Flat is
Always A♭

4th Flat is
Always D♭

Major Scale Fingerings

On this page and the next page you will find major scales, along with fingering for each hand, ascending and descending.
Scale fingerings <u>always avoid placing the thumb or fifth finger on a black key</u>.

E-flat Major Scale
DIRECTIONS: Practice each scale, hands separately, several times per day until it can be played easily and accurately. <u>Scale degree numbers are printed in red.</u> Finger numbers are printed in black. Be careful to play legato at places with the thumb under and where fingers cross over the thumb.

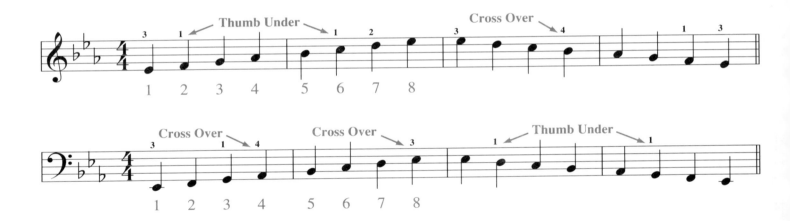

A-flat Major Scale
DIRECTIONS: Practice each scale, hands separately, several times per day until it can be played easily and accurately. <u>Scale degree numbers are printed in red.</u> Finger numbers are printed in black. Be careful to play legato at places with the thumb under and where fingers cross over the thumb.

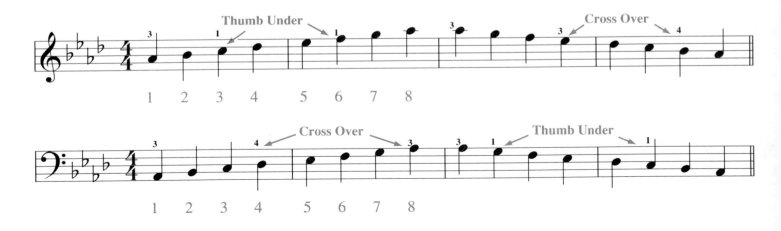

Teacher's Note: The scales on pages 24 and 25 need NOT be learned at the same time. They may be done individually, according to your preference, along with other pieces that follow. A scale may be used as a warm-up for pieces in the same key as the scale.

Key Signatures With Sharps

Sharps in a key signature are numbered from *left to right.* The sharps are always in the *same order.*

1 Sharp =
Key of G Major

2 Sharps =
Key of D Major

3 Sharps =
Key of A Major

4 Sharps =
Key of E Major

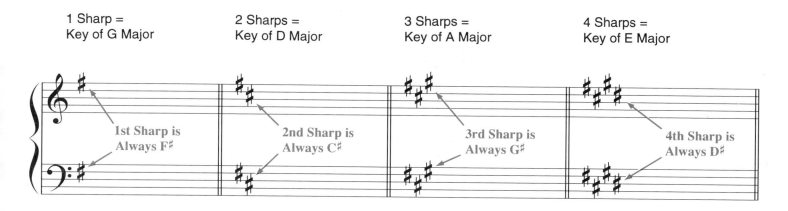

1st Sharp is Always F♯

2nd Sharp is Always C♯

3rd Sharp is Always G♯

4th Sharp is Always D♯

A Major Scale: DIRECTIONS: Practice each scale, hands separately, several times per day until it can be played easily and accurately. Scale degree numbers are printed in red. Finger numbers are printed in black. Be careful to play legato at places with the thumb under and where fingers cross over the thumb.

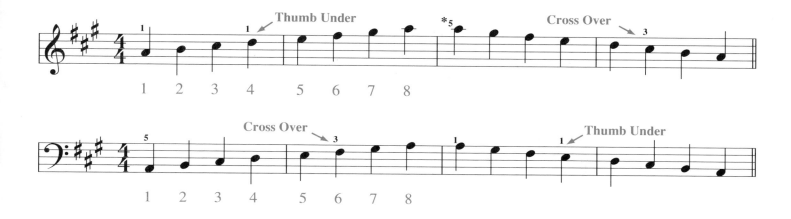

E Major Scale: DIRECTIONS: Practice each scale, hands separately, several times per day until it can be played easily and accurately. Scale degree numbers are printed in red. Finger numbers are printed in black. Be careful to play legato at places with the thumb under and where fingers cross over the thumb.

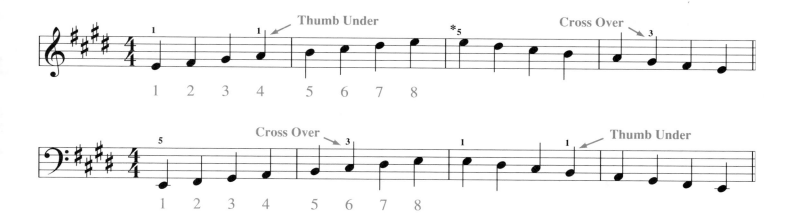

Teacher's Note: Tetrachords are purposely not presented here for sake of simplicity. Tetrachords will be introduced with the circle of keys later in this series.

* The fingering will have to be adjusted when two or more octaves are played.

Notes On a Shared Beam

Notes in different staffs may share the same beam, usually when the melody is divided between hands, as in measures 13 and 14. Notice that a single phrase mark covers both treble and bass notes.

When this occurs, it looks as if rests have been omitted. However, it is not necessary to have rests in this situation. The note values in the treble and bass are counted as if all were in one staff.

Theme from String Quartet (4th Movement) (Haydn, Op. 72 No. 2)

DIRECTIONS: Notice the 2/4 time signature. The rhythm is somewhat similar to the piece on page 9.
Be sure to use the pedal in the last seven measures.

Rolled Chords

A wavy line to the left of an interval or chord indicates that it is to be played in arpeggio style as a rolled chord. This means to quickly play the notes one-at-a-time rapidly moving from bottom to top. The bottom note is started slightly ahead of the beat so that the top note is played precisely on the beat. The notes played *ahead of the beat* are HELD as though tied into the chord, as shown in the sample.

White Key Flats

A flat sign means to play *one key to the left.* This is usually a black key, however, C-flat and F-flat are *white key flats* because one key to the left is a white key. F-flat in measure 12 is played the same as E. White key flats are sometimes used to spell intervals in music that has three or more flats in the key signature.

Green Grow the Lilacs (American Folk Song)

DIRECTIONS: Be sure to play all B's, E's, A's and D's flat as shown in the key signature. Chords and intervals to be rolled are found in measures 5, 8, 9, 12, 13 and 14. Look for accompaniment patterns that are repeated; one pattern occurs ten times.

Moderato ♩ = 100-108

Chord Inversions – Flat Keys

A **triad** is a 3-note chord made up of a **root** (lowest note) and notes at the interval of a 3rd and a 5th above the root. The chord is named after the root. The chord symbol (red letter above the upper staff) indicates the root name of each chord. When the root is the lowest note of the chord, the chord is said to be in *root position.*

An **inversion** of a triad is made by moving the lowest note up one octave (putting it above the remaining two notes). This can be done twice to form two different inversions. Where printed in red between staffs:

Root = Root Position; 1st = 1st inversion; 2nd = 2nd inversion.

Flat Key Inversion Etude (Schaum)

DIRECTIONS: Watch the clef signs; this exercise starts with both hands in the bass clef, then has two clef changes and ends with both hands in the treble clef.

The right hand fingering is the same for all root position chords, for all the 1st inversion chords, and for all the 2nd inversion chords. The left hand fingering follows a pattern which is repeated with each new chord.

The **new leger note E**, above the treble staff, is used near the end. If necessary, check the front reference page for its keyboard location.

The broken chords in the left hand follow a pattern. A *root position* broken chord is repeated three times and followed by a *1st inversion* broken chord. This pattern occurs with each chord: C, F, B-flat, E-flat and A-flat. The left hand fingering is similar for each of these chords.

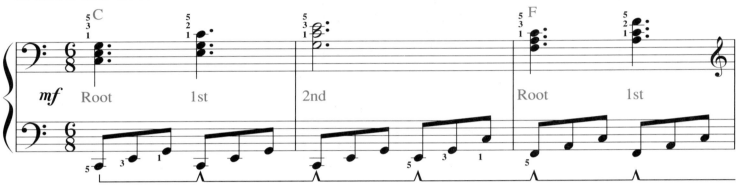

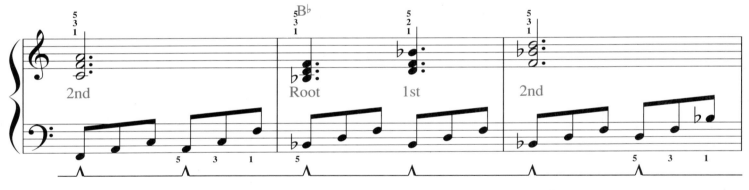

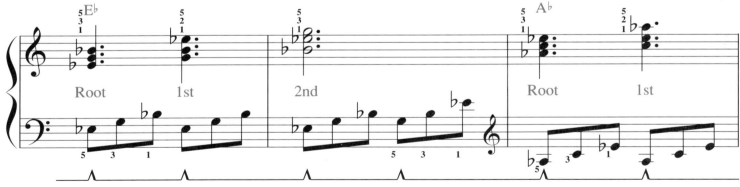

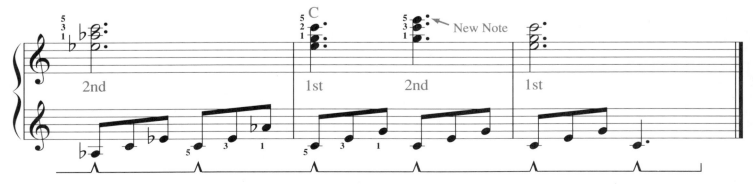

Chord Inversions – Sharp Keys
The chord symbols (red letters) indicate the root chord name. The triads and inversions are labeled in red as follows:

Root = Root Position; 1st = 1st inversion; 2nd = 2nd inversion

Sharp Key Inversion Etude (Schaum)

DIRECTIONS: Watch the clef signs; this piece starts with both hands in the bass clef, then has two clef changes and ends with both hands in the treble clef.

The right hand fingering is the same for all root position chords, for all the 1st inversion chords, and for all the 2nd inversion chords, similar to page 28.

The broken chords in the left hand follow a pattern like that on page 28. A *root position* broken chord is repeated three times and followed by a *1st inversion* broken chord. This pattern occurs with each chord: C, G, D, A and E. The left hand fingering is similar for each of these chords.

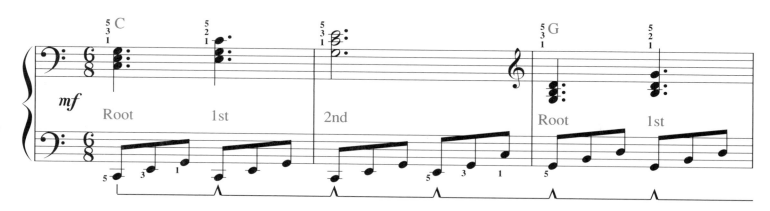

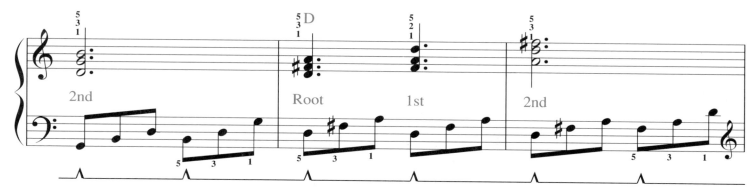

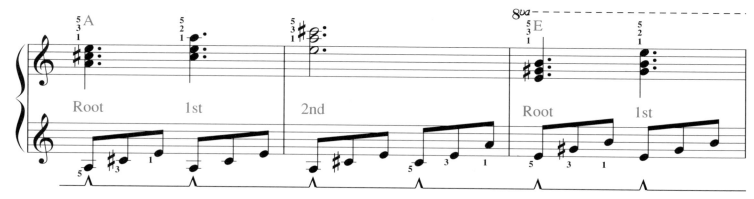

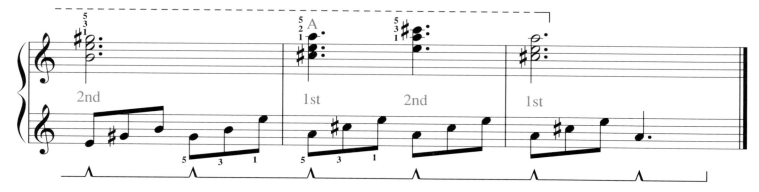

Dotted 8th and 16th Note Rhythm

A dot placed to the right of a note extends its value by one half. A dotted 8th note is equal to one 8th note tied to a 16th note. The dotted 8th note is usually combined with a single 16th note. When connected by a beam, the 16th note has a short double beam, as shown here. A dotted 8th and 16th together make one beat in 2/4, 3/4 and 4/4 time, the same as one quarter note.

Double Beam

Clementine (American Folk Song)

DIRECTIONS: At first, practice the right hand alone with a slow metronome speed until the dotted 8th and 16th rhythm is secure; then add the left hand. The counting numbers have been printed in red at the beginning of the piece.
Wait until both hands can be played smoothly before adding the pedal.

What key is this piece in? What notes must be played sharp? If you don't know, look on page 46.

There are two accompaniment patterns in the first 8 measures. A different pair of accompaniment patterns is used in the last 8 measures. The slurs help identify all of these patterns.

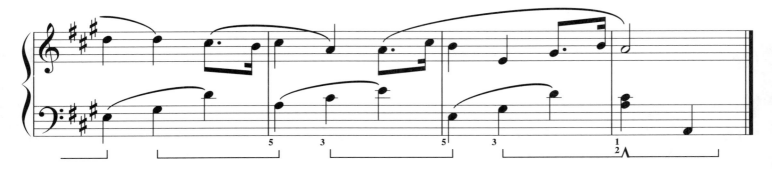

TEACHER'S NOTE: Because of different styles of teaching, the counting of the dotted 8th and 16th is optional. As a suggestion, you could use: "one-and-ah" ("ah" representing the 16th note) or "one-and-tee"; the spoken number, of course, would depend upon the number of the beat.

Two Patterns of Syncopation

The note groups shown here are common forms of syncopation. Look for them in this piece.

Go Tell It On the Mountain (African-American Spiritual)

DIRECTIONS: Watch for groups of dotted 8th and 16th notes in measures 1 and 5. Counting numbers are written in red for three measures with syncopated rhythm.

The form of this piece is A - B - A. The A section is the 1st eight measures. The B section is the second 8 measures.

Dotted 8th and 16th Notes in 3/8 Time

In 3/8 time the 8th note gets one count. This changes the note value and the way the 16th notes are counted.
Counting numbers are printed in red in the first line of music.

Rose of Tralee (Glover)

DIRECTIONS: This piece is in the key of E-flat major. Be sure to play all B's, E's and A's flat.
Notice that the first and third phrases of music are the same except for the pick-up notes.

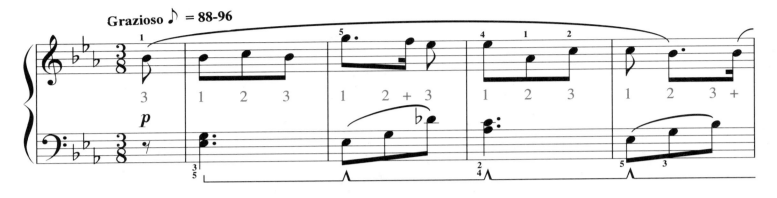

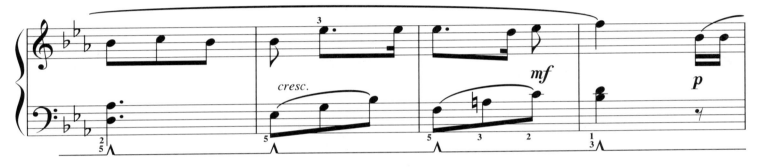

CHARLES W. GLOVER (GLOV-er) 1806-1853 — England
Glover was a violinist, theater orchestra leader and composer. He wrote many songs of which the "Rose of Tralee" is the best
known. Tralee is a small town in western Ireland, near Tralee Bay and the Atlantic Ocean. Although written by an Englishman,
this piece is familiar as an Irish love song.

Each line of lyrics corresponds to one phrase in the music:
    The pale moon was rising above the green mountain,
    The sun was declining beneath the blue sea.
    When I strayed with my love to the pure crystal fountain,
    That stands in the beautiful vale of Tralee.

Teaches Improvising an Accompaniment from Standard Chord Symbols: Schaum's **Easy Keyboard Harmony, Book 1**.

Change of Dynamic Mark With Repeat

In measure 9, there are two dynamic marks separated by a hyphen: **mp-f**. The **mp** is used when playing the first time; the **f** is used when repeating the same section.

Theme from Finlandia (Sibelius, Op. 26)

DIRECTIONS: This piece is in the key of A-flat major. Be sure to play all B's, E's, A's and D's flat.
Notice the change of finger on the bass clef note in measure 13.

Watch for the 1st and 2nd endings in the last line.

JEAN SIBELIUS (seh-BAY-lee-us) 1865-1957 — Finland

Sibelius is Finland's best known composer. "Finlandia," his most famous work, was written as an orchestral tribute to his country. After its first performance in 1900, it became the policital theme song of Finnish independence. The intense nationalistic feelings it aroused caused the Czarist government to ban some of its performances.

Sibelius is most acclaimed for his orchestral music, especially his seven symphonies. These symphonies have been recorded at various times by numerous orchestras in different countries. He is one of the first composers whose music was popularized by phonograph and gramophone recordings.

He travelled to the United States in 1914 to conduct a premiere at a music festival in Norfolk, Connecticut. During the same trip, Yale University granted him an honorary degree.

34

Chromatic Scale

The chromatic scale is a series of 12 notes that progress by *half steps.* A chromatic scale may begin on any key, black or white. The line below shows the chromatic scale beginning on C, moving up and down.

Finger numbers *above* the notes are for the right hand; those *below* the notes are for the left hand. Notice that the 3rd finger always plays every black key in right hand and left hand, up and down.

Habanera from "Carmen" (Bizet)

DIRECTIONS: The first half of this piece is in the key of C *minor.* The second half (page 35) is in the key of C *major.* Red arrows point out the notes of the chromatic scale on which the melody is based.

The triplets in measure 4 and 7 are labeled with an italic number three. Other triplets occur later in the piece, but are not labeled. Look for three notes which share the same beam.

Accent Marks

A note with an accent mark is played with extra stress or emphasis — somewhat louder than notes without accents. The loudness of the accent is related to the dynamic mark in use. For example, a small accent in a measure marked **f** will be louder than a small accent in a measure marked **p.** These are the three common accent marks:

GEORGE BIZET (bee-ZAY) 1838-1875 — France

Bizet is known mainly for his opera "Carmen," which remains one of the most popular in the entire world of opera. Oddly, its first performance in Paris in 1875 was a failure. Unfortunately, Bizet died before the successful revival in Paris, where by 1947 it had been performed 2,500 times at the same theater.

Carmen is a story of love and jealousy involving a conflict of conscience, contrasting lifestyles and violence. The characters range from wholesome, honest, simple and faithful to brazen, conniving, ostentatious and fickle. The "Habanera" is sung by Carmen in the first act, and establishes her vivacious, passionate character for the entire opera. The plot is set in Spain in the 1820's.

Bizet also wrote several other operas, a symphony, vocal, choral and piano music.

36

Cross Hand Accompaniment

In this piece, the left hand accompaniment frequently crosses over the right hand. In the first four measures there are two sets of notes in the bass staff. Notes with stem UP are for the RIGHT hand; notes with stem DOWN are for the LEFT hand.

In the first four measures, all of the treble staff notes are to be played with the LEFT hand. For these measures, the left hand counting is a combination of the *stem down* notes in the bass plus the treble notes. Therefore, there are no rests in the treble staff for the first four measures.

In the 5th and 6th measures, the melody and accompaniment return to the regular staffs, but then go back to the cross-hand style accompaniment. To clarify the movement of the melody, a dotted line has been added, connecting the melody notes.

My Heart Is Ever Faithful, from Cantata No. 68 (Bach)

DIRECTIONS: As a preparatory, practice the left hand alone, playing the notes in the bass and treble staffs with pedal, as notated. Next, play the melody alone with the right hand. Then play both hands together, very slowly at first. Be careful to subdue all accompaniment notes, especially when the left hand crosses over. The melody must always be heard clearly.

JOHANN SEBASTIAN BACH (BAHK) 1685-1750 -- Germany

A **cantata** is a vocal concert piece telling a story or play, but without costumes, scenery or props. It usually has a variety of solos, vocal combinations and choruses. The story may be sacred or secular. Bach wrote more than 200 cantatas.

Cantata No. 68 is a religious cantata with vocal parts for soprano, alto, tenor and bass, accompanied by 2 oboes, 2 violins, viola, cello and keyboard. The keyboard was probably a harpsichord or clavichord. This theme from the second movement, features a soprano solo.

Poco a Poco

Poco a poco is an Italian term meaning gradually ("little by little"). It is *always used with another term* such as crescendo, diminuendo or ritard.

When combined with *crescendo* in measure 5 it means to spread the crescendo over a longer time, in this case throughout measures 5-6-7. The term is used again in measure 13.

Jenny Lind Polka (Wallerstein)

DIRECTIONS: This piece is in 2/4 time. For a review of the counting see page 9. Watch for the D.C. al Fine at the end of the last line of music.

Notice that many of the accompaniment patterns are reused several times.

The POLKA (POHL-kah) is a lively dance for couples using small steps and hops. It is usually in 2/4 time. It was first popular in Bohemia (now part of Czechoslovakia) in the early 1800's. In the 1840's it become an enormously popular ballroom dance throughout Europe and in the United States. It remains popular to this day among many ethnic groups, especially those from eastern Europe.

38

Grace Note

A *grace note* (see measure 6) is a small note played quickly before the principal note (full size note). A grace note has *no time value* and does not affect the counting of the principal note. The principal note is played *on the beat*. A grace note may be above or below the principal note. A grace note is affected by a key signature and previous accidentals in the same measure.

Theme from Serenade in G (A Little Night Music) (Mozart, K525)

DIRECTIONS: The grace notes here should be played slightly *ahead* of the beat so the principal note is played *on the beat*.

Watch for parallel motion in the first line and again in the last line of music. A red arrow has been placed above the first repeat sign as a reminder of where the repeated section begins.

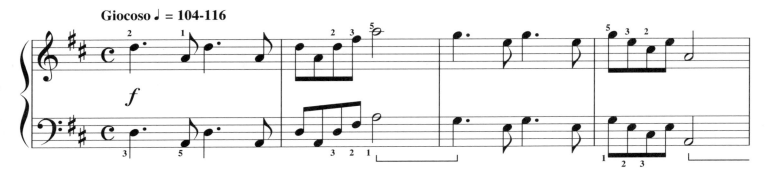

TEACHERS' NOTE: At first, it is recommended that this basic interpretation of the grace note be taught. As the student becomes more advanced, additional fine points of the grace note may be added.

Double Grace Notes

The two small notes in measure 5 are *double grace notes.* Both of them are to be played quickly before the principal note (see page 38). The principal note is to be played precisely on the second beat as shown by the red arrows. Similar double grace notes are found in measures 9, 13, 17 and 21.

It is also possible to have triple grace notes, although they are seldom found.

Theme from Serenade for Strings (Tchaikowsky, Op. 48)

DIRECTIONS: Some of the grace notes are affected by the key signature.
Be sure to play the appropriate flat where necessary.

40

Grace Note Interpretation

In this piece a grace note precedes an *interval* in the bass. The *two notes* of the interval are considered the "principal note." The grace note and principal notes are struck *together.* The grace note is immediately released and the principal notes are held for their full time value. This type of grace note is sometimes called a "crushed" style of grace note.

The style, mood and speed of the music will determine how a grace note is played. Pieces with a fast tempo or with a style that is bold, strong, vigorous or rather heavy will use a *crushed grace note.*

The Campbells Are Comin' (Scotch Folk Song)

DIRECTIONS: The accompaniment in the first eight measures imitates the drone bass of a bagpipe, an instrument commonly used in Scotch music. Be sure to "crush" the grace notes, as explained above.

Watch for the dotted 8th and 16th notes in the last eight measures. The counting numbers have been printed in red.

Evening Star from "Tannhauser" (Wagner)

DIRECTIONS: This piece is in the key of E major. The first three sharps in the key signature (F#, C# and G#) are the same as in the key signature on page 40.

Six melody notes in the first line use part of the chromatic scale (see page 34). This chromatic sequence is indicated in red. Watch for the 1st and 2nd endings.

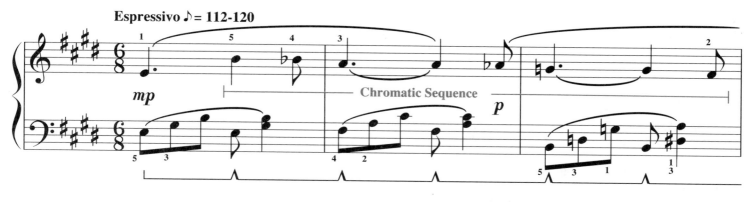

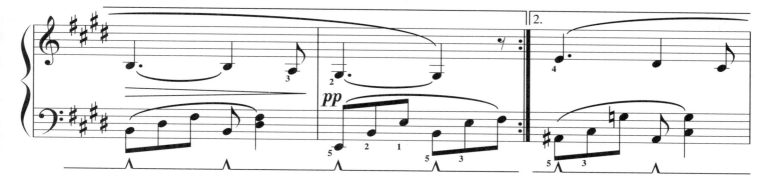

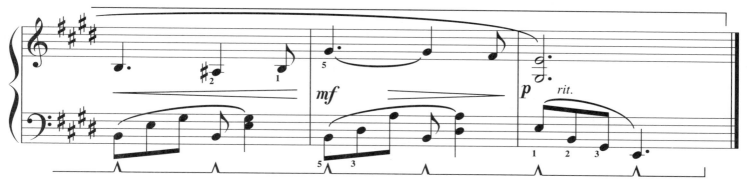

RICHARD WAGNER (VAHG-ner) 1813-1883 — Germany

Wagner's grandiose and lengthy operas were controversial when first performed and even now provoke differing opinions. By today's standards of fast-paced movies and TV dramas, the movement of the story in these operas seems ponderous and slow. It sometimes takes eight minutes for a singer to convey a simple message such as "I love you" or "Goodnight." The subject matter may appear hopelessly old-fashioned. However, this needs to be put into perspective.

Try to imagine conditions in the mid-1800's. These operas reflect a much slower pace of living. Audiences of Wagner's day were accustomed to leisurely entertainments. There was a great interest in mythology and mystical topics. Pomp and pageantry were common in European countries, where royalty and nobility still reigned. The horse and buggy was the primary transportation; railroads and steamboats were high-tech. The fastest communication was the telegraph. Automobiles, telephones, TV and computers did not exist.

"Tannhauser" (TUN-hoy-zer) is a story of the conflict of sensual and spiritual love with contrasting pagan and Christian religious values. "Evening Star" is sung in the third act, asking a blessing for the soul of the heroine, Elisabeth, on her way to heaven.

The Trill

The trill is a musical ornament performed by rapidly alternating the principal note and the note on the *scale degree above.* It is indicated by the letters "tr." written above the principal note, usually followed by a wavy line. The wavy line shows the length of the trill. Since this piece is in the key of F the upper note of each trill must be one of the notes in the scale of F major. The interval between the trilled notes may be a half step or a whole step.

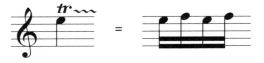

A common trill consists of 16th notes beginning with the principal note. The trill continues for the length of the principal note. Notes of a trill are affected by the key signature and by previous accidentals in the same measure.

Trill Etude (Schaum)

DIRECTIONS: The treble notes in measures 1, 3 and 5 are all to be played the same. In each case it is a dotted half-note trill. In measure 1 all the 16th notes of the trill are written. In measures 3 and 5 the trill symbol is used.

The trills in measures 9 and 11 are both for a half note but have a different principal note. The trills in measures 13 and 14 are both for a quarter note but a different principal note.

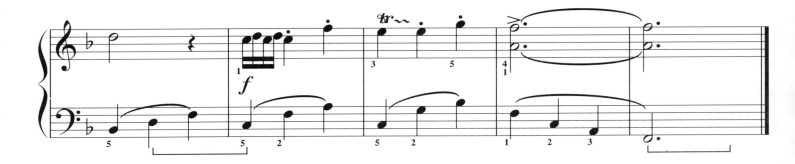

TEACHER'S NOTE: It is recommended that the student's first encounter be with a basic "measured" trill (equivalent to 16th notes) starting on the principal note, as used in this piece. Trills beginning on the upper note, as well as "improvised" or "free-style" trills may be presented at a later time as they are encountered in music of different styles and composers.

Theme from Third Symphony (3rd Movement) (Brahms, Op. 90)

DIRECTIONS: The first 12 measures are in the key of C minor. At the key change it switches to the key of C *major*. At the D.C. al Fine it returns to the key of C minor.

Look for the triplet rhythm in measure 11 as shown by the red arrow.

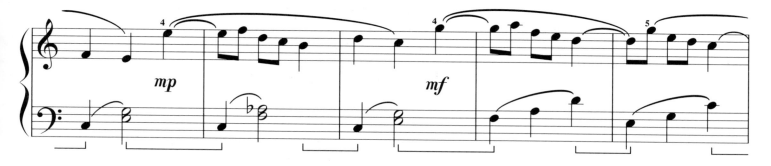

JOHANNES BRAHMS (1833-1897) — Germany
Refer to page 23 for information about this composer.

Author and Composer Names

In music with words, there are often two different names listed below the title. The author of the lyrics is listed on the *left side;* the composer of the music is listed on the *right side.* The music on this page is printed this way.

In some cases just one name is listed on the right, below the title. This means that one person has written *both the lyrics and music.*

Star-Spangled Banner

DIRECTIONS: A pair of 8th notes is used on the third beat of many measures. Be careful to play this rhythm *correctly and differently* than the dotted 8th and 16th note which also appear on the third beat of other measures. Since this is such a familiar melody, be sure you're playing the rhythm as written, not as you remember it.

Francis Scott Key (1779-1843)   John Stafford Smith (1750-1836)

STAR-SPANGLED BANNER STORY

The words for "Star-Spangled Banner" were written as a poem of four verses by Francis Scott Key during the war of 1812. The first verse is the one that is commonly sung. The other verses are rarely used.

Key was a lawyer appointed to arrange the release of a prisoner held by the British fleet in Baltimore harbor. On September 13, 1814, with a flag of truce, Key boarded a British warship and was successful in his negotiations. However, the British would not allow Key to return for fear that their imminent attack on Baltimore would be disclosed. Key was detained and witnessed the bombardment of Fort McHenry from the deck of a British prison-ship. He anxiously watched the flag at the fort. In the night sky he saw only the rockets and bomb shells, but at early dawn when the smoke and haze cleared, the sight of the flag inspired him to write these words.

The flag which flew over Fort McHenry was enormous, measuring about 50 feet in length. A replica now flies continuously over the fort and at Key's gravesite. The original flag, which contained 15 stars, is preserved in the Smithsonian Museum in Washington, D.C.

It is ironic that the music was written by an Englishman, John Stafford Smith, who originally titled it "To Anacreon In Heaven." This theme has been used as a military march, a political song, and even a drinking song. The music was combined with Key's verses shortly after the poem was written, and its popularity spread quickly. Although it was used in ceremonies by the U.S. armed forces for many years, it wasn't until 1931 that this combination of words and music was officially declared by Congress as the national anthem.

You are now ready to progress to Schaum's **PIANO FOR ADULTS, Level 4.**

MUSIC DICTIONARY

Terms not listed here may be found in the INDEX (page 48) or on the REFERENCE PAGES (Front and Rear Inside Covers).

Most musical terms are Italian, because music writing began in Italy. The accented syllable is shown in *capital letters.*

See the Front and Rear Reference Pages for illustrations of basic music elements and correlation of notes with their keyboard location.

Terms listed here are limited to those commonly found in Level Three methods and supplements. For a more complete listing get the Schaum DICTIONARY OF MUSICAL TERMS . With over 1550 words in 96 pages, it contains most terms found in program notes for recordings, concerts and newspaper reviews, including frequently used Italian, French, and German words. It is helpful in working with band and orchestra instruments, vocalists and choral groups.

---

accelerando (ahk-sell-er-ON-doh) Becoming gradually faster in tempo.

adagio (ah-DAH-jee-oh) Slow, slowly.

agitato (ahd-jih-TAH-toh) Agitated, restless.

alla marcia (ah-lah MAHR-chee-ah) March style.

allargando (ah-lahr-GAHN-doh) Gradually slower and louder.

allegretto (ah-leh-GRET-toh) A little slower than *allegro.*

allegro (ah-LEG-grow) Fast, quickly.

andante (ahn-DAHN-tay) Moderately slow; at a comfortable walking pace.

andantino (ahn-dahn-TEE-noh) A little faster than *andante.*

anima (AH-nee-mah) Spirit, life, animation.

animato (ah-nee-MAH-toh) Lively, spirited.

a tempo (ah TEHM-poh) Return to the previous tempo.

basso marcato (BAH-so mahr-CAH-toh) Emphasize the bass notes.

bravura (brah-VOO-rah) Boldness, brilliance.

brillante (bree-LAHN-teh) Brilliant, showy.

brio (BREE-oh) Vigor, spirit, gusto.

cantabile (cahn-TAH-bil-lay) Singing style.

cantando (cahn-TAHN-doh) Singing style.

chamber music Music involving a small group of performers for a small hall or parlor. Usually for various instrumental combinations from two to ten players.

common time 4/4 meter. Time signature is: ¢

con (KONE) With.

concerto (kon-SHARE-toh) Long composition for solo instrument accompanied by band or orchestra displaying the talents of the solo performer.

cresc. = crescendo (cre-SHEN-doh) Gradually increasing in loudness. Also abbreviated with the sign: ⎯⎯⎯⎯

D.C. al fine = da capo al fine (dah KAH-poh ahl FEE-nay) Return to the beginning and repeat, ending at the word *fine.*

decr. = decrescendo (deh-creh-SHEN-doh) Gradual decrease in loudness.

dim. = diminuendo (di-min-you-END-oh) Becoming gradually less loud. Also abbreviated with the sign: ⎯⎯⎯⎯

dissonance (DISS-uh-nunce) Combination of simultaneous musical sounds that are unpleasant or harsh to the listener.

dolce (DOL-chay) Sweetly, softly.

doloroso (doh-loh-ROH-soh) Sadly, sorrowfully.

drammatico (dreh-MAH-tee-koh) Dramatically.

dynamic marks Symbols and words indicating changes of loudness.

eleganza (el-leh-GAHN-zah) Elegance, grace.

energico (eh-NAIR-jee-koh) Energetic, powerful.

enharmonic Writing the same musical pitch in two different ways, such as C# and D-flat.

espressivo (ehs-preh-SEE-voh) With expression and emotion.

etude (ay-TOOD) Music study-piece to develop technical skills.

expression marks Musical terms and instructions affecting tempo, loudness and mood.

8va [When placed above] play one octave *higher* than written.

[When placed below] play one octave *lower* than written.

fff = fortississimo (fohr-tih-SISS-ee-moh) Extremely loud.

fine (FEE-nay) End.

fz = forzando (fohr-TSAHN-doh) With force, energy, strongly accented.

giocoso (jee-oh-KOH-soh) Humorously, playfully.

grandioso (grahn-dee-OH-soh) Dignified, majestic.

grazioso (gra-tsee-OH-soh) Gracefully.

larghetto (lahr-GET-oh) A little faster than *largo.*

largo (LAHR-goh) Very slow, solemn.

legato (lah-GAH-toh) Notes played in a smooth, connected manner with no interruption in sound.

leggiero (led-jee-AIR-oh) Light, delicate.

lento (LEN-toh) Slow, but not as slow as *largo.*

L.H. = Left Hand

maestoso (my-ess-TOH-soh) Majestic, dignified.

marcato (mahr-CAH-toh) Marked, emphasized.

melodia marcato (meh-LOH-dee-ah mahr-CAH-toh) Emphasize the melody notes, usually in the treble.

meno (MAY-noh) Less.

metronome (MET-roh-nome) Device to determine tempo or speed in music, measured in beats per minute.

misterioso (miss-teer-ee-OH-soh) Mysteriously.

M.M. = Maelzel's metronome. See *metronome*.

moderato (mah-dur-AH-toh) Moderately.

molto (MOHL-toh) Very, much.

mosso (MOHS-soh) Moving, animated.

non troppo (NOHN TROHP-poh) Not too much.

octave (AHK-tiv) Interval of an 8th; the top and bottom notes have the same letter name.

op. = **opus** (OH-puss) Unit of musical work usually numbered in chronological order. May be a composition of any length from a short single piece, a collection of pieces, to a full symphony or opera.

passione (pah-see-OH-neh) Passion, emotion.

pesante (peh-SAHN-teh) Heavy, weighty.

phrase (FRAZE) Group of successive notes dividing a melody or accompaniment pattern into a logical section. This is comparable to the way sentences divide a text into sections.

piu (PEE-oo) More.

poco (POH-koh) Little.

poco a poco (POH-koh ah POH-koh) Little by little, gradually.

ppp = **pianississimo** (pee-ah-nih-SISS-ee-moh) Extremely soft.

presto (PRESS-toh) Very fast, faster than *allegro*.

primo (PREE-moh) 1) First. 2) First part or player. In a piano duet the first (upper) part is labeled *primo,* the second (lower) part is labeled *secondo*.

rall. = **rallentando** (rah-lenn-TAHN-doh) Gradually growing slower.

R.H. = Right Hand

rit. = **ritardando** (ree-tahr-DAHN-doh) Gradually decreasing the rate of tempo.

rubato (roo-BAH-toh) Small slowings and accelerations of the tempo of a piece at the discretion of the performer or conductor.

scherzando (skare-TSAHN-doh) Playfully, jokingly, humorously.

secondo (seh-KAHN-doh) Second part or player. See *primo*.

semplice (SEMM-plee-chay) Simple, plain.

sempre (SEMM-pray) Always, constantly.

sfz = **sforzando** (sfor-TSAHN-doh) Sudden emphasis or accent on a note or chord.

sostenuto (soss-teh-NOO-toh) Sustained; holding notes to full value.

spiritoso (spir-ih-TOH-soh) Animated, with spirit.

symphony (SYM-foh-nee) Large piece of music written for orchestra.

tempo di marcia (TEMM-poh dih MAHR-chee-ah) March tempo.

tempo di valse (TEMM-poh dih VALSE) Waltz tempo.

tempo I Return to the original tempo.

ten. = **tenuto** (teh-NOO-toh) Sustained, held to full value.

tonic First degree of a major or minor scale.

tranquillo (trahn-KWILL-oh) Tranquil, quiet.

vivace (vee-VAH-chay) Lively, quick.

vivo (VEE-voh) Lively, animated.

Suggested SHEET MUSIC SOLOS

• = Original Form   * = Big Notes   ✓ = Chord Symbols   (All Published or Distributed by Schaum Publications, Inc.)

58-38   AMERICAN INDIAN SUITE ..... (4 Authentic Tribal Themes)
58-30 ✓ ANCHORS AWEIGH .... Zimmerman
58-31   ASPIRATION ("From Foreign Lands" Op. 15, No. 1) .. Schumann
58-39   BEETHOVEN'S 7th SYMPHONY .... (Second Mvt. Theme)
58-44 ✓ CAISSONS SONG (U.S. Field Artillery) .... Traditional
58-21 ✓ DIXIE .... Emmett
58-43 •* DRIZZLY DAY (Minor Key) .... Holmes
58-01 ✓ FASCINATION WALTZ .... Marchetti
58-41 • GHOSTLY JIVE (Minor Key) .... Leach
58-02 ✓ GIVE MY REGARDS TO BROADWAY .... Cohan
58-03 ✓ GOODBYE MY LADY LOVE .... Howard
58-42   GREASE PAINT GERTIE .... McKinley
58-07 ✓ HAVA NAGILA (Minor Key) .... Israeli Folk Dance
80-08 ✓ IN THE MOOD .... Garland
58-40 • JELLY BEAN JUMP .... McKinley

58-24   JOY PRELUDE ("Jesu Joy of Man's Desiring") .... Bach
58-32 ✓ JUST A CLOSER WALK WITH THEE .... Spiritual
58-36 ✓ LET ME CALL YOU SWEETHEART .... Friedman
58-34   MINUET IN D .... Salieri
58-11 ✓ NATIONAL EMBLEM MARCH .... Bagley
58-45 ✓ SEMPER FIDELIS (U.S. Marines) .... Sousa
80-21 ✓ SEND IN THE CLOWNS .... Sondheim
58-23 •* SKATE BOARD (Cross Hands) .... Schaum
58-12   SLEEPY LAGOON (Triplets) .... Coates
58-18 ✓ STAR SPANGLED BANNER .... Commemorative Ed.
58-49 • SUMMER SCHERZO (Minor Key) .... Leach
58-15   SYMPHONY No. 40 (First Theme) .... Mozart
58-04 ✓ YANKEE DOODLE DANDY .... Cohan
58-33 ✓* YELLOW ROSE .... Traditional
58-10 ✓ YOU'RE A GRAND OLD FLAG .... Cohan

48

INDEX